新自然主義

原來:屈原、關公、媽祖,都不是中國人

別再誤會中國!

The China you don't know

邱顯洵 著　文魯彬 譯

漫畫中國虛實光影、
解剖帝國真貌

漫畫一直是一種有如針刺的視點，在閱讀視野提供
強有力的觀照力。民主化、自由國家的出版、傳播
領域，漫畫成為符合、適應時代的視窗。其實，也
是匕首，刺向一些假面，探觸真實。

面對中國，已是世界的課題。這個亞洲大陸、有長
久歷史的國家，從古以來的不同帝國，甚至經歷蒙
古人和滿人的統治，以漢字的文化條件形塑歷史形
貌。面對歐洲經由近現代的挑戰，曾經從「夜郎自
大」到「東亞病夫」，搖晃於時代的際遇。

號稱民主革命的中華民國，建國三十八年，就被號
稱社會革命，其實是共產革命的中華人民共和國取
代，民主只是右左獨裁權力的口號。以「中華民

國」和「中華人民共和國」為名的近代中國，都在標榜近現代的口號中，浸染沉重的傳統中國文化因子，似乎無法真正成為現代文明國家。

後冷戰時期，歐美國家曾經在聯中制俄的迷思中，透過將中國當成工廠、市場的連結，讓中國走資化，引導進入世界文明秩序，但結果證明是冤枉之路。這個國家存在著戀眷強權的虛妄歷史，在「愛好和平」的面具下，隱藏著武攻文嚇的本質。

怎樣看中國？
從漫畫看中國，怎麼樣？
中國眼中、台灣眼中、世界眼中、
未來眼中，怎樣看？

《原來：屈原、關公、媽祖，都不是中國人》是一本有趣的重新觀照中國的漫畫書，漢英對照的圖說，也適合英文讀者。此時此際，是一本釐清對中國錯誤知，恢復中國原形的細膩診察報告書。

作者已出版多冊漫畫書，對台灣、對中國的歷史和
現實有深刻認識和了解，尤其以漫畫之筆、鞭辟入
裡，彷彿解剖刀一樣，撥開真相，見現實與歷史的
分明。

謹推介給閱讀者，一讀再讀，一看再看。保證不虛
此讀！

詩人、文化評論家

拆穿「中國」真面目

要正確認識中國，第一個原則就是懷疑中國共產黨政府的任何官方說辭，不管是「大內宣」或是「大外宣」都不可信。這樣才不會上當、中計被騙。第二個原則要學會區分中國政府、媒體、學界、五毛族和一般人民說法的同與異。我聽聞中國的任何看法，都是掌握上述這兩個原則去做判斷，也才能對中國的真相看出端倪。

至於了解中國過去的歷史，也一樣要有戒心，不能被國民黨或是共產黨這兩個老宿敵、新盟友所騙了。如何以當今台灣人的主體視野去瞭解中國歷史，說來真是大哉問、大課題。這本漫畫職人邱顯洵的《別再誤會中國》就是由一本透過漫畫來引導廣大讀者不要再誤入歧途，把中國歷史想錯了、看錯了，也就是他所說要去「破譯」傳統史觀的企圖。

邱顯洵的畫風帶著嘲諷，每張畫都很犀利地去揭穿過去
被扭曲、被渲染，甚至被誇大的中國史面貌。有些錯誤
的中國史觀有時是你我可能都習以為常，或許根本不知
如何去判真偽。以下就是本書揭穿的歷史迷思和假象，
很值得省思：

「中國」是居天下之中，西戎、北狄、東夷、南蠻都是
四方之「化外之民」，神聖的「中國」不就是很小嗎？
5000年歷史其實不可考，「中華民族」更是1902才被
發明出來的政治名詞。「五族共和」則是為了反清的民
國革命而虛構出來的民族主義宣傳。「炎黃子孫」更是
1937年國共兩黨為攜手抗日而創造出來的「反日」口
號。

再往古推，所謂狹義定義的古早正統中國，早在3000
年前就消失了。那麼「中國」歷史不就沒有蒙古帝國建
立的元朝和女真人建立的清朝嗎？如果把眼光放在台灣
的歷史身上，該被質疑的史觀又包括「誰是台灣人的祖
國？」、「祖國來了，是要歡迎？還是要趕快逃？」如

果孫文三次來台灣，都拿外國護照，他怎麼會是台灣人的「國父」？「中華民國」政權逃到台灣，台灣人要怎麼界定自己國家的疆界？同樣地，在李登輝前總統任內頒布的「國家統一綱領」，又倒底是要統一哪一個國家呢？

在另外兩個主題：「從世界看中國」和「從未來看中國」，也分別有生動的漫畫：諷刺月球是中國的神聖領域，中國四大發明和新四大發明；拆穿中國是愛好和平的虛假；也批判總是把百年國恥掛在嘴上的中共政權；更打破「血濃於水」說辭的背後野心。

總之，本書收錄的36幅漫畫，其實就是36則足以破除中國從古迄今諸多迷思的有力命題，值得讀者們在閱後深思。我推薦這本漫畫書給應該對中國有更正確透視的台灣人。

蕭新煌

總統府資政

Good china,
made in Taiwan?

有一年春節期間，我在時任教職的岳母家吃飯時，無意間看到碗盤的底部全以英文寫著「Good china Made in Taiwan」。我不禁笑了起來。

大寫的「China」是「中國」，小寫的「china」則是陶瓷杯碗盤等餐具。那套很實惠的碗盤是學校送老師的春節賀禮。第一時間，我覺得，想出此句的人實在蠻有幽默感的。

那時才剛解嚴沒幾年，我無法確定，這句話是否解嚴前就已經一直印在該校贈送的碗盤餐具上了。但是在往後討論到戒嚴肅殺的國民黨年代時，我腦海裡，三不五時即會浮現出「Good china Made in Taiwan」這個曾引我一笑的英文組合。有沒有可能，這句看似十分有趣的話後，藏著不止博君一笑的意涵？我自問。

「Good china Made in Taiwan」，是「好瓷器 台灣製」和「好中國 台灣製」的雙關語，前者較單純，但若是後者，解釋成「中國之美好，（純屬）台灣之內宣」，那就帶有十足反諷的意味了，若然，似亦滿符合戒嚴時代（包括「本省人」和「外省人」）的「黨外」精神。蓋「宣揚中國的無限好」配上「貶抑台灣的徹底俗」，不正是我們那一整代人的洗腦程式 ─ 亦即，所有「經驗台灣」轉化成「驚艷中國」的過程？！

當然，在那樣的專制體制下，全盤照收，甚至內化政權所灌輸的認知內容，乃正常現象，學子、人民難有反問、抗拒的可能。彼時，台灣人一生下來彷彿就已經內設了一個DNA ─ Do Not Ask！不要問！別思也別想，照單全收就對了。

然而，思想綁小腳的時代終究是一去不返了。在解嚴後的台灣，法蘭西之迪卡爾（René Descartes）「敢於思」的「我思，故我在」（Cogito, ergo sum）搭配上德意志之康德 (Immanuel Kant)「勇於知」的「放膽求知」(Sapere aude)，最終逐漸轉成「我在思故我」而面臨「台灣人到底應該如何看中國？怎麼看自己？」的大哉問。

對無法在台灣落地生根的人或政黨來說，不問則已，一問之下，此「大哉問」實乃「大災問」也 — 天上宮廷的 「大好中國美景」瞬間遭還原為人間凡塵的「景美國中好大」。何也？今日台灣人腦裡的價值、腳下的土地和心中的國族等三大認同結合之故也。

就我個人來說，毫無疑問，中國文化有它值得驕傲、光明的一面，但是，無庸置疑，也有其誇張、陰鬱的一面。而台灣與其之關係，縱是千絲萬縷，卻因拜自由民主之賜，始能為中國洗淨鉛華，為台灣撥雲見月，此不能不說是同為台灣人和中國人之幸也。

邱顯洵這本《原來：屈原、關公、媽祖，都不是中國人》諷刺漫畫書中，可說是處處醍醐灌頂，中英對照，更見視野，最終提供了讀者兩個選擇：要嘛，「別再誤會中國！」要嘛，「別誤中國，再會！」。

是為序。

謝志偉

台灣駐德代表

從認同解構到
重新建構的過程紀錄

這本《原來：屈原，關公，媽祖，都不是中國人》的漫畫書，雖剛出爐卻不能算是新書，因為書裡收集36張畫，是個人從事漫畫創作多年來與「中國」相關的創作集結。出版這麼「政治」的書，特別是觸及著敏感的國族認同，首要感謝一群有相同想法，且願意幫助出版的編輯伙伴們，還有為之作序的先進前輩們，本書以雙語付梓，除了希望以傳統紙本與網路世代對話，也顧及想了解臺灣與中國的國際讀者。

過去，中國挾其龐大外宣資源，幾乎掌控所有對臺灣的歷史解釋權，然自2019年香港反送中運動開始，到2022年俄羅斯入侵烏克蘭戰爭爆發後，國際局勢遽然進入版塊重組之變局，全球進入全新冷戰。亞太地區的臺灣，特別是飽受中國欺凌的臺灣，成為牽動國際局勢的焦點，世界需要重新認識臺灣與中國；此時重新以圖文去剖析真正的中國，希望能把常年纏繞寄生在臺灣身上，如同騰蔓似的種種歷史糾結剝去，能夠讓世界認識真正的臺灣。

記得小學五年級四月的一個下午，全校突然被長年穿著硬領旗袍，皺紋被沖刷成淚溝的女校長，用一列公車帶到孫文紀念館，每個人都被迫戴著黑紗，在啜泣聲中緩緩前進。空氣中還有一種像菊花夾著福馬林的死亡氣味，站了三個小時參拜了躺在棺材中的蔣介石，是我人生第一次看到屍體。

二十五歲時的一個冬夜，在炎熱的恆春半島軍事基地服役時，被迫半夜跪在營裡禮堂的水泥地上，奮力潑墨書寫輓聯，更在天亮前搭建出蔣經國的靈堂。

這一對來自中國的父子，在我祖先世居的土地上，跨越近半世紀，搭建起充斥著中國圖騰的電影片廠，強迫無數的楚門們，合力演出一齣至今仍難以落幕的悲劇。

一直到二十七歲我終於離開，到一個必需要重新認識自我的異國，過去深信不疑的種種信仰開始崩塌，甚至覺得自己是處在一種自我放逐的飄浮狀態。這種掙脫謊言追尋真實的過程，要用很長的時間，去走過一種浮士德式的自我認同洗滌，用筆墨從迷惘中探索出圖像，再型塑出一個完整且堅定的國族認同。這本漫畫應該解讀為從認同解構後重新建構的全程記錄。

為什麼是三十六張？三十六不是什麼密碼，只是想向江戶時代的浮世繪大師葛飾北齋，其巔峰代表作「富嶽三十六景」致敬，當時七十歲的畫家要如何敘述一座在日本人心靈的聖山？這對畫家是的極大考驗，北齋花了四年時間，揹著畫具行囊，以雙腿或牛車扁

舟，不同季節、不同視野，以崇敬及熱愛，創作出
日本美術史上最經典作品。

同時也深深影響了這個世界，畫出富士山的永恆我
不揣淺陋也想學習北齋，用畫一座山的心情試圖以
繪畫來詮釋出臺灣的國族形狀，三十六只是一個起
點。

From identity deconstruction to identity reconstruction

This graphic narrative "The China You Don't Know ", although just released, cannot really be considered "new" as it brings together 36 illustrations related to "China" that I have created over the years. This is a "political" book, and thus quite sensitive – particularly given its associations and implications within the context of national identity. As such, the work owes a great deal to the like-minded members of the editorial/ publishing team, as well as to the trail blazing "elders", some of whom contributed introductions to this work. In addition to the traditional print and electronic formats, we have made the text bilingual to accommodate international audiences who want to gain a better understanding of Taiwan and "China".

For decades "China" has used its massive propaganda machine to control almost entirely discussion and interpretation of Taiwan's history. Recent events, however, such as the 2019 anti-extradition uprisings in Hong Kong, and the outbreak of the Russian-Ukrainian war in early 2022, indicate a tectonic shift in the international situation.

With this new cold war comes a focus of international attention on the Asia-Pacific region generally, but more particularly, on the incessant bullying of Taiwan by China. The world needs to re-understand Taiwan and China. We hope that analyzing the real China through graphics and text such as this publication will help strip away the tangle of historical falsehoods and enable the world to learn about the true situation.

One April afternoon when I was in the fifth grade of primary school, our stiff-collared cheongsam-attired headmistress, with tears staining her wrinkled face, ordered the entire school onto a string of buses headed for the Sun Yat-sen Memorial.

Everyone was forced to adorn black mourning bands as they plodded forward amidst the sound of sobbing and cries of regret. The air was heavy with the stench of death-laced with chrysanthemums and formaldehyde. I stood for three hours to pay homage to Chiang Kai-shek lying in his coffin – the first time in my life that I saw a human corpse!

At the age of twenty-five, stationed in sultry hot southern Taiwan during my military service, I was forced to kneel through the night on the concrete floor of the camp's auditorium, splashing ink and writing elegiac couplets that were to be used to adorn the funerary rites for Chiang Kai-shek's son Chiang Ching-kuo.

So, for nearly a half a century this father and son duo from China, essentially constructed a film studio full of Chinese totems on the land of my ancestors, forcing countless entrapped Taiwanese "Trumen" to play out a tragedy that even to this day has not ended.

I existed within this "set" and believed it to be reality until, at the age of twenty-seven, I found myself in a foreign country and at last was able to review all that had transpired in my life. The ensuing collapse of all those deeply held beliefs and unquestioned assumptions transported me to a state of mind that seemed as though I was floating in a sea of self-exile.

This process of breaking free from lies and pursuing the truth takes a long time, and for me it involved a kind of Faustian reevaluation of my identity, a reevaluation involving my use of pen and ink to retrieve images from a morass of confusion in order to reshape a complete and firm notion of identity. The text and illustrations of this narrative is really a record of the complete breakdown and deconstruction of my identity followed by the process of reconstruction.

Why thirty-six illustrations? Thirty-six is not a mysterious code, rather it is my way of paying tribute to Katsushika Hokusai, the master painter and print maker of Ukiyo-e in Japan's Edo period, specifically his masterpiece "Thirty-six Views of Mount Fuji". How would this seventy-year-old artist portray this great

Preface

mountain that occupies such an important place in the hearts and minds of the people of Japan?

To meet this test of greatness Hokusai spent four years carrying his painting equipment and travelling by foot, ox cart or boat, throughout the different seasons, and observing from all different perspectives, all the time with respect and love, creating the most classic and influential artistic works not only for Japan but for the entire world.

It may seem presumptuous, but I aim to learn from Hokusai's eternal images of Mount Fuji, using the spirit of portraying such an iconic mountain to interpret the form and content of Taiwanese identity. This collection of thirty-six interpretations is merely a point of departure.

A 從中國看中國
China Looks at China

瞎子摸象式的認識中國　030
Everyone thinks they know China,
but who really knows China?

以老子肚臍為中央的國度　032
A country centered around one's navel?

Contents

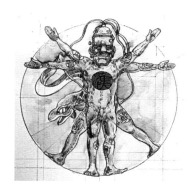

B 從台灣看中國
Taiwan Looks at China

Contents

C 從世界看中國
Taiwan Looks at China

Contents

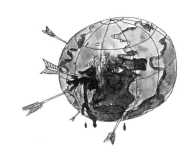

D 從未來看中國
Looking at China from Future

Contents

A

從中國看中國

China Looks at China

瞎子摸象式的認識中國

中國是什麼？中國有多大？
歷史有多長？中國在那裡？
中國是敵人？

中國是祖國？我可以不當中國人
嗎？我是中國人嗎？

全世界應該找不到一個國家像台
灣一樣，一個國家認同那麼多元
的國家了。

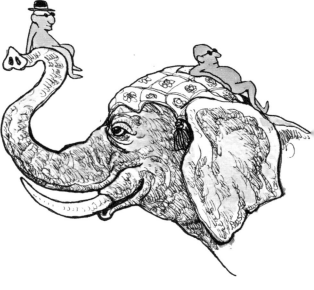

Everyone thinks they know China, but who really knows China?

What is China? How big is it? How long is its history? Where is it? Is China my enemy?

Is China the mother/fatherland? Can I not be a Chinese? Am I Chinese?

There can't possibly another country where the people have such a diversity of opinions about their identity.

Everyone thinks they know China, but who really knows China?

以老子肚臍為
中央的國度

「中國」字面意思是「中央之國」，最早出現在
公元前11世紀的青銅器上。當時周朝的人心目中
其統治的國家「居天地之中」而環繞在外的民族
是「居天地之偏」稱為「四夷」。

北狄

山西

Xia 夏 河南

東夷

南蠻

A country centered around one's navel?

The Chinese characters for "China" literally mean "middle kingdom" or "country at the center" and first appeared on bronze implements dating from the 11th century BC.

At that time, the rulers of the Zhou Dynasty believed that their country or kingdom was nested or "resided in between heaven and earth", whereas the peoples residing in the periphery or even outside of this kingdom were collectively known as the "four barbarians".

中華人愛掛在嘴上的「華夏」

Chinese people love to call themselves "Chinese"

吹噓出來的古國

四大文明古國最初是梁啟超提的，他在其寫於1900年的《二十世紀太平洋歌》中，認為「地球上古文明祖國有四：中國、印度、埃及、小亞細亞是也」。其實這種自吹自擂的說法是有爭議的。

The Blustering Boast of being an "Ancient Country"

Four ancient civilizations were first mentioned by Liang Qichao, "20th Century Pacific Song" written in 1900: "there are four ancient civilizations on earth: China, India, Egypt, and Asia Minor." Actually this self-aggrandizing view is highly controversial. [Translator's note: the Chinese character for "blowing on a cow" mean to boast, hence the depiction of the oxen.]

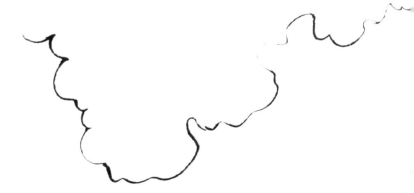

「地球上古文明國有四，中國、埃及、印度、羅馬是也！」
《廿世紀太平洋歌》1900 梁啟超

"There are four ancient civilizations on earth: China,
India, Egypt, and Asia Minor." Liang Qichao, 1900 "20th
Century Pacific Song"

1902年才被發明的「中華民族」

中華民族五千年的說法是完全沒有科學的證據。全然是政治上的需要而被製造出來的。

The 1902 Myth of "Chinese Nation"

There is absolutely no scientific evidence to back the claim that the Chinese nation is five thousand years old.

This narrative was created entirely out of political necessity.

1921年「炎黃子孫」才出現

黃帝及炎帝都是遠古的傳說……而炎黃子孫是人造的共同想像。

1937年對日抗戰前夕國共兩黨代表共赴陝西共祭黃帝陵「炎黃子孫」正式出櫃。

The 1921 Myth of "Descendants of Yan and Huang"

Huangdi and Yandi are ancient legends known to most people of Han ethnicity as the common ancestors. But again, this is a product of imagination and expediency. In 1937, on the eve of the war against Japan, the representatives of both the Nationalist and Communist parties went to Shaanxi to jointly pay tribute to the Yellow Emperor's Mausoleum, and thus was the myth born.

黃帝和炎帝這兩個傳說人物
能生下子孫也是種神話。

The two acient legends, Huangdi
and Yandi, is able to give birth to
descendant is another myth as well.

發明中華民族的男人

中華民族，是一個在晚清被梁啟超發明的近代化政治概念，其思想是按照中國民族主義建立國族，統合中國境內所有民族並樂見其一體化，在此之前，世界上沒有中華民族這個民族。

The Man Who Invented "The Chinese"

At the time of its invention by Liang Qichao in the late Qing Dynasty, the idea of a Chinese nationality was a then-modern political concept. The idea was to establish a nation based

on an ethnic Chinese nationalism, and use this to unify and integrate all the other ethnic groups in China. Prior to this time the world knew of no such thing as a nation of ethnic Chinese.

五族被迫共和

「五族共和國」源自清末立憲運動的「五族大局」，是中華民國成立初期的政治口號，也是所謂的「中華民族」被創造出來的理論根據。

A Republic Forced Upon the "Five Races"

The coming together of the "Republic of Five Nationalities" that is the basis for the so-called" ethnic Chinese" originated from the "Five Races Under One Union" constitutional movement in the late Qing Dynasty.

真正中國早在三千年前就滅亡了

中國第一個有文字記載的朝代，有金文及甲骨文的正統華夏早在3,067年前就被蠻族周給滅亡了！

The real China perished 3,000 years ago

China's first dynasties with their own inscriptions on gold and bone included the real Chinesewas destroyed by the barbarian tribe known as the Zhou as early as 3,067 years ago!

牛頭馬面，是中國神話中兩個陰間的神祇。

Ox-Head and Horse-Face are two guardians of the underworld in Chinese mythology.

	On the left: you've been dead and gone for a long long time!
**	On the right: Sir, you went out as the emperor of the Shang dynasty!

歷史中沒有元朝

西元1206年忽必烈稱帝。1271年定漢文國號為「大元」，稱為大元大蒙古，定都「大都」。

由蒙古人建立的是大蒙古帝國（The Great Mongol Empire），當時的中國只是在蒙古鐵蹄下滅亡的無數國家之一。

There was no Yuan Dynasty in the history of China

In 1206, Kublai Khan proclaimed himself emperor. In 1271, the Chinese characters for the empire was "Da Yuan" of the Great Yuan, and was called the Great Mongolia of the Great Yuan, and the capital was "Khanbalik" or Da Du in the Chinese pronunciation. The Great Mongol Empire was founded by the Mongolians, and China at that time was just one of the countless countries that perished under the iron hooves of the Mongolians.

* 大宋王朝（Song Dynasty）

歷史中沒有清朝

純為建州女真人的愛新覺羅氏以十七萬的人數統治了一億多人的中國，建立了達268年（1644－1911）的政權。

There was no Qing Dynasty in the history of China

Rather, this "China" was a reign of 268 years (1644-1911)by group of 170,000 people from Manchuria known as the Aisin-Gioro Nurhaci who governed more than one hundred million people.

B

從台灣看中國
Taiwan Looks at China

誰是祖國？

Who is the "Fatherland"?

祖國來了

「祖國來了，快逃！」Eric John
Ernest Hobsbawn 1917-2012馬克
思主義史學家霍布斯邦在經典之作
「十九世紀三部曲」中，引述一位
義大利農婦對兒子所說的話。

論述當時「祖國」、「統一」之
名，行侵略併吞壓制人民之實的歷
史情境。

英國歷史學家艾瑞克‧霍布
斯邦，研究馬克思主義的著
名學者。

Eric Hobsbawn, an
English historian, well
known for studying the
Marxist.

The Fatherland is Coming

"Run away, the fatherland is coming"
Eric John Ernest Hobsbawn 1917-2012.
In his classic books about the "long
nineteenth century", the Marxist historian Hobsbawn quotes an Italian
peasant woman speaking to her son.

He discusses the historical situation
whereby the "fatherland" and "unification" were used as pretexts to sup-
press the actual situation of aggression abroad and oppression at home.

祖國又來了！

祖國應該是對自己母國認同的稱謂。

在中文卻是用字義解釋為「祖先的國家」，尤其在台灣移民社會，國民黨流亡政權教育部解釋祖國即為「祖籍所在的國家」。

況且，台灣為了不斷更換的「祖國」，在每個時代中都付出慘痛的代價。

我們還需要「祖國」嗎？這是英國歷史學家艾瑞克‧霍布斯邦（Eric Hobsbawm，1917-

| 馬克思（Marx）

2012）在他的著作《帝國的年代》裡，引用一句義大利農婦的話，描述打著「祖國」名義侵略與壓迫的情境。是流傳至今的名言。

而霍布斯邦是研究馬克思主義的著名學者。而馬克思本身是非常厭惡國族主義的，他主張無產階級無祖國。

B: Which one is it this time?

這次是那個祖國？

快逃！祖國來了～

A: Run away quickly, the fatherland is coming…

Scappa! Che arriva la patria~
Run Away the fatherland is coming~

The British historian Eric Hobsbawm (1917-2012) in his book "The Age of Empire", famously quotes an Italian peasant woman who is telling her son to run away lest he be caught and conscripted by the government – an illustration of aggression and oppression in the name of "homeland". Hobbsbon was a prominent scholar of Marxism, while Marx himself was very critical of nationalism, advocating that to the proletariat there is no such thing as a motherland.

半路相認意外的國父

孫文去世後被中國國民黨奉為「國父」，完全是封建意識及政治需求，與真正歷史不符。孫文一生來台三次，都是持外國護照入境。

1. Fundraising
Sep. 28, 1900
Japan-Taiwan

2. Transit
Early Aug. 1913
Shanghai-Fujian-
Guangdong-Taiwan-Japan

Fake Founding Father?
Mistaken Founding Father?

Following his death, the Chinese KMT held up Sun Yat-sen as the "Father of the Nation". This feudal approach, driven by political expedience was totally inconsistent with historic facts. Sun's three visits to Taiwan were all on foreign passports.

3. Transit
Late May 1918
Guangzhou-Taiwan-
Japan-Shanghai

Sun Yat-sen: "Hmmm. I wonder why Taiwanese consider me to be the father of their nation?"

驅逐韃虜的賓拉登

一生崇尚暴力的孫文，1895年武力攻擊官府。
1912年暗殺不聽命於他的革命黨人也暗殺新聞
記者，其革命口號為「驅逐韃虜」證明他是個
恐怖首腦。

恐怖份子：孫文（孫逸仙）懸賞1000銀元。

Reward 1000 Silver Yuan for terrorist
Sun Yat-sen aka Sun Yi-shien

Bin Laden Drives Out the Barbarians

Sun, was a lifelong advocate of violence. He used force against the Qing government in 1895, and in 1912 assassinated members of his party who disobeyed and even assassinated journalists. His revolutionary slogan "Drive Out the Barbarians" proves the mind of a terrorist.

袁世凱才是國父

1921年創建中華民國的國父是袁世凱。

但1940年3月21日,國民黨常務委員會決議,尊稱總理孫中山為國父。

Yuan Shikai: the Real Founding Father of the Republic of China in 1921

On March 21, 1940, the Central Standing Committee of the Chinese KMT resolved to honor chancellor Sun Yat-sen as the father of the nation.

*Yuan Shikai (1859-1916): I'am China's George Washington, the real father of the nation.

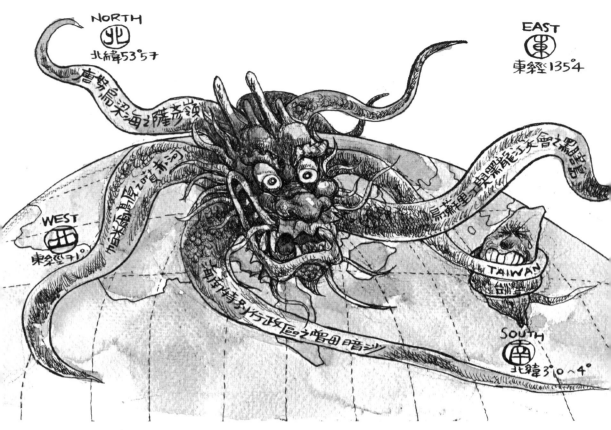

中華民國的疆界？

在2005年，行政院新聞局所發表之〈中華民國年鑑〉曾規定疆域領土四極點為：

極東：合江省撫遠三角洲烏蘇里江和黑龍江合流之黑瞎島，東經135°4'；
極西：新疆省瓦罕帕米爾高原之噴赤河，東經71°；極南：南海特別行政區曾母暗沙之立地暗沙海域，北緯3°10～4°；極北：蒙古地方唐努烏梁海之薩彥嶺嵴，北緯53°57。

Republic of China Territory?

At 2005, For a time "The Republic of China Yearbook" published by the (now defunct) Government Information Office of the Executive Yuan stipulated four territorial coordinates as: 135°4' east which is where the Ussuri River and Heilongjiang River join in the Fuyuan Delta of Hejiang Province (Bolshoy Ussuriysky Island); 71° east location of the Panj River in the Wakhan Pamir Plateau, Xinjiang Province; 3°10-4° north - Hainan and James Shoal Special Administrative Region; and 53°57 north - the Sayan Mountains of the Tannu Uriankhai in Mongolia.

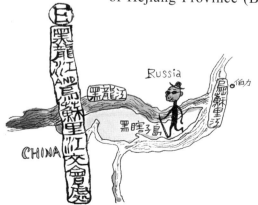

① 1890－1889

黃龍旗 李鴻章監造

Yellow Dragon Banner,
by Li Hongzhang

② 1911－1912

湖北共進會的

鐵血九角十八星旗

Jagged Nine Corners
Eighteen Star Flag, by
the Hubei Joint Progress
Association

③ 1912－1928

五色旗
Five-color flag

①

②

③

青天白日旗？
真正的中華民國國旗是五色旗

Five-colors is the National Flag

④ 1928 - 1949

青天白日旗

Blue Sky and
White Sun Flag

＊KMT re-
porting to the
Founding Fa-
ther: The Party
Flag is now the
National Flag!

⑤ 1949 -

五星旗

Five-star flag

國歌
是卿雲歌

中華民國創立後臨時政府頒布「五族共和歌」作為臨時國歌，

之後兩度以卿雲歌譜曲作為國歌。

現在被稱作國歌的，是國民黨辦軍校黃埔軍校訓詞譜曲。

1929年成為國民黨黨歌，1937年國民黨通過以黨歌作為國歌，同年國民黨政府通令適用。

The Song of Auspicious Clouds from the Third Century B.C. is the National Anthem!

When the Republic of China was established the interim government provisionally adopted the song "Five Races Under One United Nation" as the national anthem. Later the "Song of Auspicious Clouds" from an ancient Chinese text was twice made the national anthem.

What is now called the national anthem is composed of lyrics and music a training ditty of the Huangpu Military Academy which was a military academy run by the Kuomintang. In 1929 the Kuomintang adopted it as their party anthem, and in 1937 the Kuomintang resolved to make the party anthem the national anthem. Later in the same year, the Kuomintang government issued an order making this the national anthem.

1945年國民黨到台灣後，看電影要起立唱國歌，一直到1990年才逐漸廢止。

陳定南擔任宜蘭縣長時，率先廢除這項規定。感謝陳定南！

In a movie theater, on screen, it shows Army Officer Academy at the top and San Min Zhu Yi (Three Principles of the People), our aim shall be…… at the bottom.

One of the audience, "Stand up to sing the national anthem!"

Beginning in 1945, before watching a movie, concert, etc. everyone had to stand up and sing the national anthem. It was not until 1990 that this gradually began to be phased out. Thank you Chen Ting-nan!

國統綱領的出山

1990年代總統李登輝為了安撫統派，成立國家統一委員會，訂出一套國家統一綱領。

1996年台灣民主已發展至直選總統，國家統一只是少數人的囈語。

2006年2月27日，陳水扁總統主持國安會議中決定國家統一委員會終止運作。

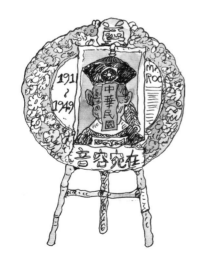

Birth of the Guidelines for National Unification

In order to appease the unification faction, in 1990 then President Lee Teng-hui established the National Unification Committee and formulated a set of national unification guidelines.

By 1996 however, Taiwan's democracy had developed such that there were direct elections of all legislators and the president; "national reunification" was just a rant of a small minority.

The guidelines ceased to function with the presidential decree made by Chen Shui-bian on 27 February 2006 while presiding over a meeting of the National Security Council.

C

從世界看中國

Taiwan Looks at China

自古曾屬於我
就永遠是我的

帝國的主張已是歷史。世上曾有很多帝國，甚至有橫跨歐亞非的日不落帝國。

用自古屬於我國為理由侵略別國早就是被淘汰的觀念了！

It's been mine since time immemorial, it will always be mine!

Claims of empire are relegated to history. There have been many empires around the world, even empires spanning Europe, Asia and Africa upon whose territory "the sun never set". But invading other countries on the grounds that those territories "rightfully belong to our country since ancient times" is a concept that has long been eliminated!

①大英 British Empire 1766~1956 33671萬平方公里

②大漢 The Han Empire BC 202~220 1500萬平方公里

③阿拉伯 Caliphate 632~1258 1340萬平方公里

④亞歷山大 Alexander Empire BC 336~323 550萬平方公里

⑤蒙古 Mongolian Empire 1206~1529 3300萬平方公里

⑥羅馬 Roman Empire BC 27~1453 590萬平方公里

⑦波斯 Persian Empire BC 550~334 695萬平方公里

中國人的世界觀

共產黨式的世界觀是誰拳頭大就聽誰的。

The Chinese View of the World

The Chinese communist version of weltanschauung or "world view" is simple: "might makes right"!

* Uncle Sam: "Chairman Xi that's enough, no need for more punching!"

**Xi: "What's your problem? They will listen to whoever has the biggest fist!"

太陽自古屬於中國

從中國古書記載，太陽星君日宮天子、羲和、東皇太一、炎帝、日主，都是統治太陽的神明。So，太陽當然是中國的。

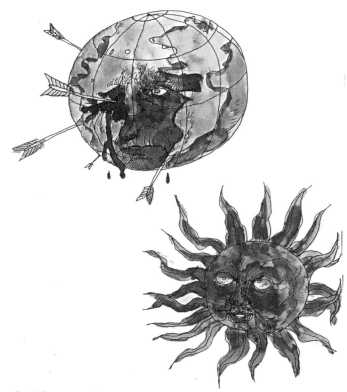

Since Ancient Times the Sun Has Belonged to China

The sun has belonged to China since ancient times. According to ancient Chinese books, the emperor, Xihe, Emperor Taiyi, Emperor Yan, and the Lord of the Sun are all gods who rule the sun. So, the sun is of course Chinese.

廣寒宮
The Plaza where
Chang'e lives.

Since Ancient Times the Moon Has Belonged to China

The moon is China's sacred sphere In the Xia Dynasty from
the 21st century to the 17th century BC, Hou Yi, who shot
the sun, and his wife, Chang'e, were sent
to the moon to garrison for more
than 4,000 years.

月球自古屬於中國

西元前21世紀～17世紀的夏朝有位射日的后羿其妻嫦娥
派往月球駐防已經4000多年了。

由左至右：印刷術、造紙術、火藥、指南針。

Illustrated (left to right): Printing technology, Paper manufacturing, Gunpowder, and Compass.

為政治服務的四大發明

1942年蔣介石約見李約瑟。第二年不負重託的李約瑟在重慶提出造紙術、印刷術、指南針和火藥為中國古代「四大發明」的說法。

The invention of
"The Four Great Inventions of China"

In 1942 Chiang Kai-shek met with the scholar Joseph Needham to entrust him with a mission. Two years later Needham came up with the "Four Inventions" for Chiang.

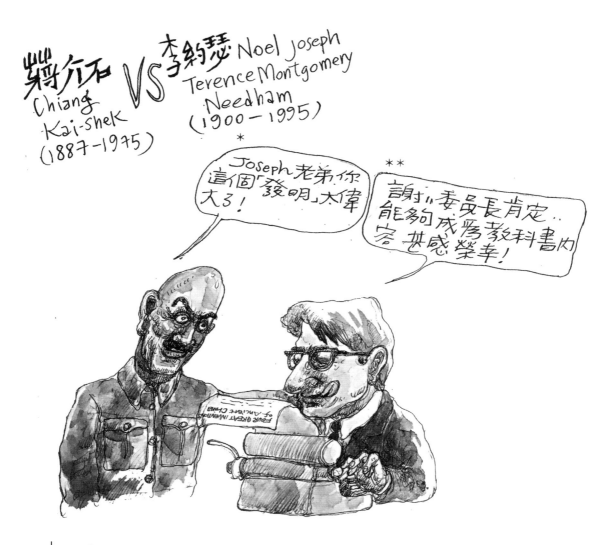

* Chiang: "Joseph old buddy, this invention of yours is really something!"
**Needham: "Thank you Generalissimo for your affirmation,
   it is a great honor to have this included in all the textbooks."

把地球管起來

毛澤東：「把地球管起來！讓全世界都聽到我們的聲音。」

1955年毛澤東對新華社負責人說的話，今日以毛的傳人自居的習政權正在往此方向邁進。

To Rule the Earth

Mao Zedong, "Rule the Earth! Let the entire world hear our voices." This is what Mao Zedong said to the head of Xinhua News Agency in 1955 Today's Xi regime, the self-proclaimed successor to Mao, continues to move in this direction.

Mao Zedong: "Rule the Earth! Let the entire world hear our voices."

林默娘、關羽和屈原

「中國」歷史五千年？關羽是蜀國人，林默娘大
宋人、屈原是楚國人，他們可都不會認為自己
叫做中國人。

What is your country?

Five thousand years of Chinese history? Really? Three
revered historical figures Guan Yu, Lin Mo-niang
and Qu Yuan would hardly consider themselves
"Chinese".

① The Dragon (symbolizing the emperor) addressing three historic generals:

② Guan Yu (Han era circa 220): "I am of the Empire of Shu Han"

③ Lin Mo-niang (Northern Song circa 960): "I am of the Great Song Dynasty"

④ Qu Yuan (Warring States circa 300 BCE): "I am of the State of Chu"

從未來看中國

Looking at China from Future

普天之下莫非王土

「普天之下」在詩歌中的原文是「溥天之下」，《說文解字》解釋「溥，大也」。

「溥天之下，莫非王土；率土之濱，莫非王臣；大夫不均，我從事獨賢」。正確解釋為：天下的土地，都是王治下的領土；管理一方土地的諸侯，都是王的臣子；同為王臣，卻勞逸不均，唯有我的差事特別的繁重辛苦。其表達的是抱怨之情。

將抱怨之語扭曲為肯定當權者擁有無上權力的語句，是中共扭曲原文本義、欺騙閱讀中文的人。

Under the heavens there is no land that does not belong to the emperor

As an example of how the Chinese use language to control thought, the first character or word of this ancient poem from the Book of Odes has been changed from "great" or "huge" to "universal" and the original text of the poem is really an expression of complaint by the author on account of the uneven and unfair distribution of duties.

It is the Chinese communists who twist the meaning of the original text deceiving people who read Chinese into thinking what is actually a complaint to be a statement affirming the supreme and unassailable power of the Chinese government.

「愛好和平」的中國

中國共產黨宣稱愛好和平,卻發動病毒戰爭、
資訊戰、經濟侵略、債務支配、種族清洗、
邊界衝突、網路攻擊、南海、東海、臺海惹事。
這種「和平」是世界的公敵。

Peace-loving China

While the Chinese Communist Party claims to love peace, they launch virus wars, information attacks, economic aggression, debt domination, ethnic cleansing, border conflicts, cyber-attacks... just look to the South China Sea, East Kazakhstan, and Taiwan Strait to see how China is the common public enemy pitted against the rest of the world.

中國戰狼對內宣傳強調「雖遠必誅」

China's Wolf Warrior style of internal propaganda emphasizes that "all must be punished, no matter how far away".

中國和平崛起，全球膽戰心驚。

China's "peaceful rise" has brought trembling with fear of war throughout the world.

Pictured: Pangu, the creator of the universe.

強國崛起

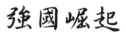

Peaceful Rise No Election

你的哈奴曼變成我的孫悟空

中國從來不是文明輸出地區而是輸入區。

從明朝神怪小說西遊記可以證明，若把佛經印度神話抽離，

中國四大小說的西遊記完全解體消失。

The Monkey's China Belt Road Initiative

China has never been an exporter of culture, rather it is an importer. The Mind era novel "Journey to the West" can demonstrate as without the Indian stories the book completely falls apart. The monkey – Sun Wu-kung is just a localized name for the Hindu god Hanuman.

哈奴曼（Hanuman），印度史詩《羅摩衍那》中的神猴，猴頭人身，勇敢機智，力大無窮，被稱為印度戰神。他曾解救阿逾陀國王子羅摩（Rama）之妻悉多（Sita），與羅剎惡魔羅波那（Ravana）大戰。

Hanuman is the monkey god in the Sanskrit epic "Ramayana" (the literal meaning is "Rama's Travels"). Having head of a monkey and the body of a human, albeit with four faces and eight hands, Hanuman is brave and clever, and extremely powerful. Riding through the clouds, Hanuman sets fire to the Langka Palace, steals the herbs of the immortals, and helps the protagonist, King Rama of Ayodhya, to defeat the demon Ravana and rescue his wife, Sita.

百年國恥何時了？

1900年的大清帝國腐敗愚昧，縱容了殘暴的拳匪。八國聯軍的軍事行動間接導致共和中國的誕生。中國國族主義竟然還拿來當萬用遮羞布。

A Century of Hate and Vengence?

The Qing government of 1900 was corrupt and ignorant, even condoning the cruel Boxers. The invading foreign armies were indirectly responsible for prompting the birth of the Chinese republic, with the new found Chinese nationalism becoming an all-purpose salve for the humiliation suffered for so long.

巨嬰之國的領導人

如此窮兵黷武的巨嬰卻又自誇：中華民族沒有稱霸基因、中國是是世界和平的建設者。

《巨嬰國》是中國心理諮商師武志紅所寫的書，2016年出版隨即被下架。巨嬰指的是身體已經發育為成年人，而心理發展卻停留在嬰兒階段，「都在找媽」，認為全世界都要聽自己的。書中直指中國「多數國人，都是巨嬰，這樣的國度，自然是巨嬰國。」

習近平是「巨嬰」的典型代表：明明只有小學文化程度，在十年文革浩劫後的平反運動中補償式的混了一個清大特權專班的學歷，偏要假扮成學富五車的博士。

The Giant Baby's Leader

The giant baby of destitute soldiers boasts that the Chinese people lack the no genes for hegemony, and that China is a builder of world peace.

"Giant Baby Country" is a book written by Chinese therapist Wu Zhihong. As soon as it was published in 2016 it was immediately censored and taken down from all shelves.

The metaphor of a giant baby refers to a body that has developed into an adult, but retains the psychological makeup of an infant constantly "looking for its mother." The is direct in its judgment of China, "when most

people are just babies in fully grown bodies, such as China, that country's style and demeanor is naturally one of the giant babies."

Xi Jinping is a typical "giant baby": everyone knows his level of cultural sophistication is that of a primary school student although he was able to use his privileged status to scrounge up a mixed a degree from Tsinghua University during the rehabilitative movement following the ravages of the ten-year Cultural Revolution.

中華文化就是將少數民族華化

在中國的少數民族發展公式就是漢化。

漢化也稱中國化、華化，是指將其他非漢族的語言文字，

同化成以漢族為主題的「中華文化」。

Chinese localization/ Sinicization Machine

The formula for the assimilation of indigenous peoples, or "Sinicization," is the same on both sides of the Taiwan strait, referring to the assimilation of all non-Han languages and culture into "Chinese culture."

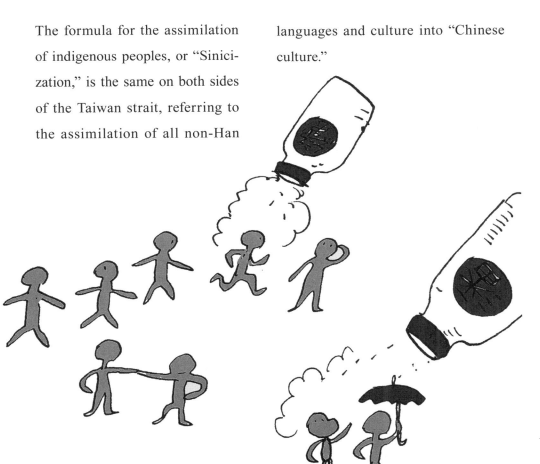

血濃於水

當代國家認同，從來不需要血緣來背書，
中國的國族的血緣論是落伍又愚昧的霸權思想。

Blood is thicker than water

The modern concept of national identity has never been based
on blood ties. China's "national blood theory" is outdated and
simply a fatuous excuse for hegemony.

從世界史裡尋找
被誤解的真相

真正的藝術家總是冒著危險去推倒一切既存
的偏見，而表現他自己所想到的東西。

————————————————————————奧古斯特·羅丹
Auguste Rodin

本書一開頭引用雕塑大師羅丹這句話，不是要表達
本書內容在藝術成份裡的想像力，相反的，要呈現
的是，從世界史裡尋找出一種長期被誤解，經過宏
觀的史料比對與思辯而得到的圖像觀點。

《原來：屈原、關公、媽祖，都不是中國人》，這
本書的出版，其實是整理自己跨越二十幾年來的國
族認同的足跡，用自己最熟悉的漫畫創作形式，以

36張漫畫集結成一本《原來：屈原、關公、媽祖，都不是中國人》的圖像創作記錄。

國族認同（National Identity）是人對於其國家或民族的歸屬感，並將國族視為一個凝聚整體的概念。知名政治學者法蘭西斯・福山（Francis Fukuyama）在〈為何國族認同重要？〉（Why National Identity Matters）一文認為，國族認同始於對國家統治正當性的共同信念，可以被具體化為訂定官方語言或是教育一國歷史的法律制度規範，國族認同也延伸到文化與價值的領域。

而臺灣對國族卻有著特別的認同分歧，特別是在頻繁的大小選舉中，立場都會成為陣營之間勝負的關鍵；儘管臺灣人會用一種鄉愿式的總結，最常聽到一句「甭擱講啦，拼經濟最重要啦！」，然而避談就能解決國族認同爭議了嗎？

用統獨擺兩邊，維持現狀這種駝鳥論述去困惑選民，也許暫時會奏效，如此混淆的國族認同歸納起來，是因為我們的不同世代有嚴重的分歧。因為對中國的認識，來自不同的時間及不同的知識源頭，即使在臺獨派的理論裡，雖說目標接近，卻也是百家爭鳴，混亂中也只能各自表述。

我在創作手繪臺灣人四百年史的五、六年期間，有幸親身受教於臺獨大老史明先生，他算是個成長於日本殖民統治時代。從「祖國派」出發的左派革命家，他對「祖國」自然有深厚的歷史情感，加上他自身在華北紅色革命陣營的生命歷程，以致我們在溝通過程中察覺出因世代而產生截然不同的觀點。儘管這段經歷不影響我們最後的創作成品，卻讓我體會到，臺灣世代需要更多的溝通，對國家的想像才能夠更完整。

這種建構過程需要時間的發酵熟成，然而從2019香港反送中，到治港國安法落實，一直到2022俄國侵略烏克蘭的戰爭來看，臺灣其實已經沒什麼逃避的空間與時間了。

Postscript

特別是中國當今紅色帝王習近平，從2012年就提出了實現「中國夢」、復興中華民族的使命。中國官方將其解讀成「中華民族的偉大復興」。「民族復興（national rejuvenation）」這個詞本身有正面意義，任何國家都有通過和平手段實現復興的權利，然而中國官方對於這一口號的解讀卻讓人背脊發涼。

因為中國所謂「中華民族偉大復興」內涵所強調的「中華民族」，從範圍上講包括56個民族。但凡曾經在歷史上與中國有過藩屬主從關係，曾受到華夏文化影響，甚至只要有某個中國神話或傳說記載過的對象，似乎都可被列在復興清單。這種民族復興的理念有著令人不安的歷史前例，特別是那些並不想被復興融到中華民族懷抱的弱小的國族，如不順從可能會付出慘痛的代價。

更何況中國偉大復興中，還有對近代因積弱而被列強欺凌的記憶，有著強烈復仇雪恥的意味。

全世界所將面臨的一個危險的問題是，要到何時中國才將覺得達到就偉大的復興了呢？是恢復到哪一個朝代？還是哪一場征伐呢？

過去民主選舉儘管用擱置統獨，維持現狀這種駝鳥論述去麻痺選民，卻往往都能奏效，然面對中國這個與臺灣歷史上糾纏不清的強國，我們必須更了解什麼是中國，才能尋找出適合的共生共榮之道，然而中國的定義是什麼？

相關論述早就汗牛充棟，但用系統性的圖解並不多見，所以自己不揣淺陋選擇以畫表述。本書用從臺灣看中國，中國看中國，歷史看中國，未來看中國的四個觀看角度，用筆墨描繪出我們一直誤會的中國真實面貌。只有按圖索驥，在圖文交織的脈絡裡，完整認識到所謂「中國」。

1996年，剛剛過世的彭明敏教授競選首屆民選總統時，我參與文宣團隊設計出鯨魚圖像來代表海洋國家的臺灣，其中有對中國過去的再解釋與對臺灣未來的新想像，至今也已過26年，2022出爐這36張圖，應該算是鯨魚的增訂條文吧！

這本書想讓對中國這個名詞心存疑惑的人獲得一些釐清，特別在中國霸權主義興起、美中關係改變，牽動了國與國關係重整之時。過去幾乎被消失的臺灣則重回舞台，但若世界上想重新認識臺灣，卻只能透過過去與現在的僵化的文件觀點，這是臺灣的遺憾，也是世界的損失！

Uncover the Long-held Misunderstanding of World History

The true artist risks all manner of danger to overthrow all prejudices in order to express that which he imagines. —— Auguste Rodin

The quote from Rodin is not meant to convey this book's imaginative artistic content. Rather it is to present the big picture of historical facts, thereby facilitating the reader's acquisition of certain perspectives on long-held misunderstandings of world history.

"The China You Don't Know" is actually my attempt to sort out the shadows and footprints of my own national identity spanning a period of 20 years. I use a medium with which I am most familiar – graphics, and have assembled thirty-six works along with narrative to produce this book.

National identity is a person's sense of belonging to a country or ethnic group and at the same time it can also be seen as a unifying concept for the particular country or group. Renowned political scientist Francis Fukuyama in his article "Why National Identity Matters" argues that a country's national identity begins with a common belief in the legitimacy of its national governance, which in turn may be embodied as legal and systemic norms that define the official language or the teaching of a country's history - national identity also extending to culture and values.

Postcript

Taiwan is particularly divided when it comes to national identity. This is especially apparent during our frequent national and local elections. A particular stance on national identity often becomes the determinant of victory or defeat. Yet, although the Taiwanese voters talk about many identity-related issues, the overwhelmingly most commonly heard phrase is "ahh, forget about that, the most important thing is the economy!" Thus, the issues of national identity continue to be sidelined – a situation not conducive to reaching a solution to this national "identity crisis".

Basically, the voters with their "independence vs unification" mentality avoid the national identity issue like ostriches burying their heads in the ground. While this approach is "effective" as far as it goes, and effective for the moment, the people remain perpetually confused, with a multitude of causes of the confusion whether it be due to different generations, different messages from different sources, or even about different Chinas!

Even among the proponents of independence, although their goals generally coincide, there are "a hundred schools of thought contending", and in the chaos it is left to each group to have their own interpretation. I had the good fortune to work with Mr. Su Beng (9 November 1918 – 20 September 2019) for five or six years illustrating his work on The Four Hundred Year History of the Taiwanese. Su, a veteran of Taiwan independence was a leftist revolutionary who grew up in the era of Japanese colonial rule but started his activities from the "motherland". He naturally had deep historical feelings for the "motherland", which was enhanced by his experiences with the red revolutionary camp in North China.

During our collaboration, completely different viewpoints regarding identity and other issues came to light. No doubt some of this could be attributed to generational differences. Although this did not adversely impact our final collaborative work, it brought home to me the need for all generations of Taiwanese to improve dialog in order to constructively reimagine our country.

Postcript

This dialog and imagination take time to process and develop. However, from the 2019 Hong Kong anti-extradition protests leading to implementation of the Hong Kong National Security Law to the 2022 Russian invasion of Ukraine, it is apparent that Taiwan may have neither the time nor room.

This is especially apparent from Xi Jinping - China's current "red emperor's" proposed mission since 2012 of realizing the "Chinese Dream" and "rejuvenating the Chinese nation". The official Chinese interpretation is "the great rejuvenation of the Chinese nation." The concept expressed by the words "national rejuvenation" itself has a positive meaning, and every nation and people should have the right to pursue rejuvenation through peaceful means.

However, the official Chinese interpretation of the slogan sends chills down one's spine. The "Chinese nation" emphasized by so-called "great rejuvenation of the Chinese nation" includes 56 ethnic groups. Many of which historically had a tributary or vassal relationship with China, but were just incidentally influenced by Chinese culture, or were mentioned in literature or historical records while retaining their own identity.

But under the Chinese scheme of the "great rejuvenation" these nations are all on the Chinese "China" inventory list. Also, this idea of national rejuvenation has many disturbing historical precedents, especially for those weaker nations that may not want to be "revived" into the embracing arms of the "Chinese nation". And those that may not choose to go along, should expect to pay dearly for their "intransigence". What's more, to this great renaissance of China clings the bitter memories of the Chinese of their own bullying by foreign powers during China's time of weakness – there is certainly an air about this rejuvenation movement that China of modern times may be seeking vengeance for the shame it suffered in the past.

A most serious question then is: at what point will China feel that it has achieved its "great rejuvenation"? Which dynasty does it seek to restore? Which conquest does it seek to reprise?

Postcript

These fractures are particularly apparent during the regular democratic elections held on the island. The identity issues continue to be ignored, voters and candidates alike choosing expediency and hiding from the issues like ostriches.

China is a powerful country entangled in the history of Taiwan. We need to better understand China if there is to be any hope of finding a suitable path to co-existence and co-prosperity. But one asks: What is China?

The debates and discussions have gone on endlessly, but very few systemic approaches to the issue have emerged. Through my illustrations and narratives, I have chosen to express four perspectives: viewing China from Taiwan, viewing China from China, viewing China from history, and viewing China from the future. Using pen and ink I attempt to describe the true face of a China that we have always misunderstood.

In 1996 I was a member of the design team supporting the presidential campaign of recently deceased Peng Mingmin (1923-2022). Our team devised a whale image to represent Taiwan as a maritime country – itself quite a reinterpretation of China's past while at the same time a new imagination of Taiwan's future. Twenty-six years have passed since then. Perhaps we can consider the 36 images of this book released in 2022 as additions to the whale design!

My intention with this book is to help people who are confused about the term "China", especially following

後記

Postscript

the recent surge in Chinese hegemony and the change in US-China relations – a change in global state-to-state relations. The recently "out of sight/out of mind" Taiwan is once again back on center stage. The world wants to renew its acquaintance with Taiwan. I hope this book can supplement the rigid, dry and stolid historical documents and current accounts: failure to better understand Taiwan's identity and "China's" reality will not only be a tragedy for Taiwan, but also the loss of a great opportunity for the rest of the world.

丘邱顯洵
Nicolas Chiou

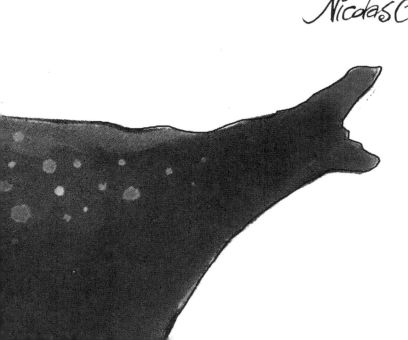

阿兜仔淺談台灣

我曾擔任太魯閣國家公園志工，除了帶團解說（主要是應當時的新聞局或外交部的要求為外國貴賓和遊客服務）以外，大部分工作就是將中文的解說資料翻譯成英文。與大多數翻譯人員一樣，我會使用一些網路上搜尋的資料。

有一個常用的是美國中央情報局CIA的「世界概況」。我在查找一些資訊時，發現他們對台灣人很不了解——網站上是這樣寫著「漢族……超過95％，土著馬來－波里尼西亞人 2.3％」，讓我非常不以為然。

而依據林媽利醫師團隊以及其他國內外學者對於台灣種族構成的研究，表明佔多數的「漢族」 台灣人中，七八成有台灣原住民血統；而其他許多漢人其實也是華南原住民的後裔（例如白越）。既然如此，為何不乾脆直接說「台灣人民／族裔群體接近100%為原住民」呢？因此，我曾寫信給CIA，指出以上所述的事實。

但沒人理我，也從來沒有接到他們的回音。

從小我就對中國語言和文化著迷。我叔叔在哥倫比亞學習「東方語言學」，我喜歡去他家看那些看不懂的中文書籍。我那美國「垮世代」（60年代初）的大哥也很喜歡閱讀《易經》、阿蘭·瓦茨（Alan Watts）論道教、和埃茲拉·龐德（Ezra Pound）翻譯的《論語》。我第一次接觸中國的學術課程是「晚清民初思想史」課程，內容涵蓋鴉片戰爭，直至中華人民共和國成立…也被置入了一些似是而非的元素。

還好，從第一次來台灣（1977年1月）至今，在台灣的每一天都有很多驚喜，也逐漸切深了解台灣與中國的區隔。45年來，我還沒去過中國（如果香港和澳門不算），雖然曾經計劃要去，但因為還有更多台灣的面貌每天不斷發現中，實在沒時間去中國。

有機會參與並翻譯邱顯洵的《原來：屈原、關公、媽祖，都不是中國人》英文版，是一個愉快的過程。讓我可以重新觀察到許多像上述的中央情報局概況所反映的「心態」，以及數十年主流「虛假信息」的遺緒。即使在今天，我仍然經常聽到生活在台灣者說「我們中國人……」而不是「我們台灣人……」；甚至到現在還在說「全省」，而不是「全國」。

我認為這本書非常有助於釐清台灣意識混亂狀態。謝謝邱先生，謝謝出版社，謝謝台灣。台灣萬歲。

American-Taiwanese Talks About Taiwan

Many years ago, I did a lot of volunteer work for Taroko National Park. In addition to being an interpreter (mostly for foreign visitors at the request of the old "GIO 新聞局" or

Postscript

Ministry of Foreign Affairs) , I translated the interpretation signs from Chinese to English. As with most translators, I had a number of special resources on the internet.

One of my most frequently relied upon resources was the US Central Intelligence Agency's "World Factbook" which in the section on the people of Taiwan/People/Ethnic groups stated something like,"Han Chinese...more than 95%, indigenous Malayo-Polynesian peoples 2.3%"

I took exception to this and wrote to the CIA pointing out the work of Dr. Lin Ma-li and others on the ethnic make-up of the Taiwanese that indicates a significant majority, i.e., 70-80 % of the "Han Chinese" in Taiwan have indigenous Taiwanese blood while many others are descended from indigenous peoples of southern China, e.g., the Yueh (aka Bai Yue), so why not just say "100% indigenous"?

I never heard back.

From an early age, I was fascinated by Chinese language and culture. My uncle studied "oriental languages" at Columbia and I used to be fascinated by the Chinese books in his library. My oldest brother during the "beat" era (early 60s) in the US liked to read the I Ching, Alan Watts on Taoism and Ezra Pound's translation of the Confucian analects. My first academic exposure to China was a course on "intellectual history of the late Qing and early Republic", covering the Opium Wars up to establishment of the People's Republic of China.

Since first arriving here in January 1977, every day is a surprise from Taiwan for me. I have yet to visit China (Hong Kong and Macau don't really count), and while I once had plans to go there, there is so much more of Taiwan that I am discovering daily so it is unlikely I will ever make it to China.

Joining in the process of creating an English version of Nicolas Chiou's book "The China You Don't Know" has been an enjoyable opportunity to look at many issues that are the vestiges of the kind of mentality reflected in the CIA Factbook

Postscript

and the result of decades of mainstream "disinformation". Even today, I still often hear the phrases like "we Chinese…" rather than "we Taiwanese…." or even "the whole province" rather than "the whole country". Even after all these years, we should know better.

I think this book will contribute to Mr. Chiu's already impressive record of helping to "set the record straight". Thank you, Mr. Chiou and the publisher. Long live Taiwan!

Robin Winkler

國家圖書館出版品預行編目資料

```
原來：屈原、關公、媽祖，都不是中國人
／邱顯洵著 . -- 初版 . -- 臺北市：幸福綠光，
2022.05
    面；公分　中英對照
ISBN 978-626-95078-9-4（平裝）
1.CST: 中國史
610                         111000251
```

原來：屈原、關公、媽祖，都不是中國人

別再誤會中國！

The China You Don't Know

作　　者	邱顯洵	英文翻譯	文魯彬
社　　長	洪美華	責任編輯	莊佩璇、謝宜芸
美術設計	謝宜芸、古杰	封面設計	盧穎作

出　　版　幸福綠光股份有限公司

　　　　　台北市杭州南路一段 63 號 9 樓

　　　　　(02)2392-5338

　　　　　www.thirdnature.com.tw

E - m a i l　reader@thirdnature.com.tw

印　　製　中原造像股份有限公司

新　　版　2022 年 05 月

郵撥帳號　50130123 幸福綠光股份有限公司

定　　價　新台幣 420 元 (平裝)

總 經 銷　聯合發行股份有限公司

　　　　　新北市新店區寶橋路

　　　　　235 巷 6 弄 6 號 2 樓

　　　　　(02)2917-8022

ISBN 978-626-95078-9-4